STANDING ALONE,
LEANING AGAINST

JIM FRIEDMAN & DAVE SMITH

STANDING ALONE, LEANING AGAINST

Coverstory books

First published in paperback format by
Coverstory books, 2022

ISBN 978-1-7397660-5-4

The cover was designed by Ian Gouge © 2022
and is based on a photograph taken by
Penelope Jane Smith © 2022.

www.coverstorybooks.com

Contents

Jim Friedman

Between the Two of Us

Dave Smith

✸

JIM FRIEDMAN

In memory of John

History

Tankas for New Year's Eve, 2020

The moon has circled
my house. Planetary cogs
turn and turn about
suburbia where I'm trenched,
reluctantly a hermit.

Near total darkness.
Neighbours sleep. I break up ice
on the water-bowl.
Air is knife-sharp on my face,
grave-cold. I hurry back in

where my cat's asleep
on his chair by the hot stove,
curled round his long dreams
on this isolated ark,
my small effort at control.

The air's full of risk,
even here - particulates
from raking the ash.
Out there, weariness and fear
of an invisible life.

That full moon, setting
behind branches, resembles
a Christmas bauble
no one could bear to take down -
one tired hope left on the tree.

History

A scullery and down the yard,
a spidered toilet, dark
as the home-built Anderson
trenched in the garden, curved, green sheets
of iron roofing it.

Gran had the softest, wrinkled skin
I'd kissed, and bunions
in supple, windowed leather shoes
moulding her swollen feet. I heard
Mother call her Mother.

Gran's legs were bowed, a wish-bone arch,
tan-coloured stockings rolled
like doughnuts or small life-buoys round
her ankles, showing white, veined legs.
She cackled when she laughed.

His oval-sided, inlaid box
Grandad offered as a joke
for me to take a pinch of snuff,
its reddish-brown like cinnamon,
placed just behind his thumb

then sniffed. And sometimes he would sneeze,
wiping his hairy nose
with large, red-spotted handkerchiefs
pulled from his pocket's leather trim,
like a clumsy magician.

My name's the same as his,
an uncle's, too, a picture of him
on their wall in uniform,
a sailor lost at sea. He looked -
I see - like mother did.

His name was spoken differently;
like silver lifted up
to see it brighten, then put back
against blue velvet: sadness
with the plush still proud.

Say *snuff, pease pudding, sculleries*,
words current in their world,
like *puttees* - Grandad photographed
on leave, with Grandma and their boy,
dressed in a sailor-suit.

Red racer

Red, metal, rubber-tired pedal car
driven through tamped-earth alleyways
and, later, trafficless, suburban streets
the shire-horsed rag-and-bone man visited.
Brick villas, subdivided, starting to go down.

Red racer, tinny chariot of fire,
my arrows of desire went no further
than the pavements of surrounding streets
obscured by fogs, save for that tail-light red
of joy there rubying my childhood.

Putting my foot down meant forwards,
reverse was digging in my heels.
I puzzled over lefts and rights that changed
when I turned round the other way.
Perspective my first inklings of an I.

Short-trousered, plimsolled, slightly dirty me,
furiously pedalling my bright red car
without an engine save my grubby legs,
my heart its fuel. Those simple journeys -
lefts, straight-on and rights, always stop at red.

Away

Maybe he's truanting from life -
the urgencies of being eight,
in others' care, not yet his own.

At first he walks then starts to trot,
footing what could be a stone
kerb to kerb, zig-zagging the street.

The yawn and stretch of morning
gathers him, seems to lighten him,
as though he's dancing down the road,

entirely verb - trot-kick-trot-kick -
and now and then a little hop,
joy in his body jumping out.

And for a while he is his own,
not knowing it, just there inside
his eyes, his elbows, on his toes -

a boy, his fetters lightly worn,
not noticed yet, their tendrils soft,
still growing, easily broken.

Trust

He threw himself off the shed roof
five maybe six times, his father
catching him, throwing him up in the air,
both laughing as he put him back
to practise one more time, just one
more go at being unafraid.

He must be fifty now, at least.
Perhaps his kids when little also dived
three feet. When he did I was tutting
even as I laughed to see such fun
run away with father and son.
Sometimes the boy cried when it stopped.

Jumping over the moon out there,
he knew what it's like to free-fall
and be caught; experienced the trust
that love between them opened to, a door
the boy unhesitatingly
ran through, his father looking up

to save him, reaching out his arms.
As if the world said 'Come' and urged
the boy, while dad stood ready to embrace
him as the future surely heading down.
Such falling, little Icarus,
to something bigger than your dad.

Parents

His love was like an aquifer,
its waters only surfacing
when crisis cork-screwed it to rise:
suddenly a shiny-eyed face
providing water for a thirst.

Hers, a river you could drown in,
carried out too deep, sucked down
by living through us. Sacrifice
her way of showing that she cared,
encouraging white-collar hopes.

The world they influenced was me,
two sisters and successive dogs.
Like taps, light-switches, they were there
at arms-length, parents on and off,
their weather built-in to the walls.

I see them differently now.
Bickering and separateness
seem like two rival tugs, each side
that rusty coaster *Family*,
gently nosing it out to sea.

Three of us with one-way tickets
on our maiden voyage,
always waving goodbye to them -
two tugs off-shore, now small enough
to see as life-boats set adrift.

Mother

1. *Clown*

She was small, a cockney, good-humoured - rude
jokes delighted her, always good for a laugh.
War-time on the box would put her in the mood
for reminiscing: East End tales of half
of nothing - chance of further learning
blocked, the books and uniform would cost
too much. Fifty years later, that turning
her down hardened her voice. That early frost
mushed hopes for better (like wanting me dressed
in a white collar instead of a blue).
Good things came to her as hand-me-downs,
like her sisters' clothes, kept for Sunday-best
at the back of her wardrobe, as you do,
when your face is not your own but a clown's.

2. *Then*

There were few Sundays to wear your best,
away from home, in service, living-in
as maid to haughty women. Your protest
was to quit. Then a crap job beating tin
deafened you. Then the small memento-box
you once showed me - for the baby who died.
You'd just finished knitting his cap and socks
when war's unravelling then pushed aside
your marriage. Then uncertain widowhood:
"missing in action" on a telegram,
so soon after your boy, you'd barely grieved.
Then you met father. The two of you stood
together through a life more spam than ham,
loyal and rancorously undeceived.

3. *Dementia*

In your last months there was little laughter.
You died as a child in my sister's arms.
You were hard on her but she looked after
you, going downhill, the brake off. The harms,
the shames she kept you from. The love she hoped
to prove; to be your good girl now, your friend.
Incontinence and violence, she coped
with stolidly on her own. At the end,
like Doctor Who on a flying visit,
you were time-travelling. Dementia meant
enjoying gravy-pie-and-mash somewhere
in nineteen forty, meant asking "Who is it?"
when she made tea, meant a long accident,
with you among the wreckage, dying there.

4. *Goodbye*

Mother: the word now is a little ark
sailing me home to you in my mind's eye.
Sitting in your chair as it grew dark,
you said "I love you" when I said goodbye.
There you were, a planet, and I your moon,
pulling away. My orbit brings me round,
back to you on that final afternoon
when, just briefly, your clear light shone. You clowned,
of course, getting me laughing like a drain.
It felt like coming home once more to tea
for two, for just us two, in our time-out
from history. Then you went walkabout,
asked if father was dead, didn't know me.
As I left, you said "I *love* you" again.

5. *After*

With hindsight now I hear that emphasis -
that *forte* on 'love' when you said goodbye -
as strangely urgent like a sudden kiss
on the cheek, as though you knew you'd soon die
and feared a mother's love was not exempt
from being taken for granted, feared that
familiarity might have bred contempt
for it, something outgrown, become old hat.
Was that what I heard - implicit reproach,
so understated as to be in doubt?
Or did you see it as the only approach
possible between us, that reaching out
over a lifetime, revisiting love
like something obscured we now had to prove?

6. *There*

Jig-saw pieces: one who lived standing still,
made a home, stayed there and kept it going
through all the necessary years until
your children left, all without you knowing
any greater happiness than theirs.
Your own - a tidy house, a cigarette
to soothe regrets, distract from mundane cares,
day-trips to see me, an occasional bet.
Regrets, what were they, mother? Who were
you in that other life you never had?
What did it feel like then, just being 'there'?
Invisible? In limbo like someone
outgrown, but not let go; prompted to sad
smiles of welcome when noticed by your son?

Late

Her indoor face is pale and cold,
vacant-looking in the shadows
of a blue, winter afternoon
becoming darker still. The old
woman shines like a risen moon.
Hands crossed on her stomach, she stares
at nothing as the daylight goes.
Her whispering sounds like prayers,
welcoming daily ghosts who come
and go about the house like grey,
slow driftings of nostalgic rain.
Sitting still, happy to roam
across the years, she lets today
rattle by like a distant train.

Together

Togetherness

The clematis involves the rose
supporting it. They slowly climb
together, tangle and enclose
each other's branches over time.
Their thorns and tendrils grow
as one, impossible to part,
but blue and crimson flowers show
two kinds of blood flow through its heart.

This was a paradigm for us
living together for years on end,
both of us learning to be close
and separate too - sinuous
enough to slowly twist and blend
stars of clematis, swirls of rose.

Accident

His tyre got caught in the tram-tracks.
Cut eye, dislocated shoulder,
fauve bruises, bent specs, in A&E
for hours - everyone patient, kind.

Shoulder re-set, they let me see him.
As we shared thankful platitudes,
his cut opened; blood tasselled down,
as if an enormous relief

poured out of him in a red sigh,
just as we were about to leave.
A little glue and he was put
together again, as we were.

Sideways

Having done the done thing - courting, marriage,
much later, kids ("your father was so chaste")
then the years of mourning camouflaged
as her depression and his overtime,
(mourning for hopes they didn't quite believe) -
they came alive in separate dreams,
ruefully indulged in quiet moments
between performances as one
more couple who had found their rainbow's end
together, alone in different rooms.

He fantasised a looser life, escaped
from suits, civilities, gymnastics
working out a life of fitting in,
assimilating to suburbia.
An elsewhere than his gated house,
his dream was Gaugin-colourful
among Pacific islanders,
all of them in nothing but sarongs.
Outdoors, beachcomber kind of life,
toes sensuously dipped in turtled sands.

Escaped from her oppressive liberty
where servants did the useful work,
she dreamt herself a farmer's wife, with lambs
calves, babies, anything that needed her,
her man's keen hungers in the bouncy bed
icing the cake of her well-risen dreams.
Big boned, florid, flirting with the hired men
felt good and made her husband act
more mindfully than when she played
her teapot-hostess-'I'll-be-mother' role.

I see them, two giraffes, stretching sideways
towards the fenced-off leaves just out of reach,
while all too wary of the lion-fierce
proprieties that kept them vigilant,
behaved, just dreamers of their wished-for lives
of louche flamboyance, home-made joys.
There is a kind of courage living down
to others' expectations when the cost
is costive: public diligence of face,
a life-long diet of the nearer leaves.

Bruise

He orders at last, just for one.
His mood seems to have turned blue
staring at the damask cloth.
A plate of food
wings like a colourful moth
to the small table set for two.
He doesn't touch his mobile phone.

He looks over where diners halt
before they're seated, then turns
away, pours more white wine and drinks
a mouthful of glass.
Difficult to say what he thinks,
as he traces first degree burns
on his grilled steak and rubs in salt.

He slowly wrings the pepper-mill,
scattering a gritty crush of scorn.
The evening seems to have uncorked
a bitter genie.
Clearly something hasn't worked
its magic. He leaves peppercorn
specks, glints of salt, a crumpled bill.

Sour dough

Hope is yeast in the air,
spongily expansive
starter, its mushroom push

taking in a white breath,
gluten alveoli
doming to a soft lung.

A leisurely air-bag
you have sprinkled with salt
tears, like a night-pillow

whispered to when all else
fails. How you expected
life to rise and greet you

with its gifts, hearts like bowls
of hope that slowly yeast
small Bethlehems of bread.

Maybe Ithacas, too -
loaves with more crust than crumb,
more rise than good for them.

Happiness

As though coming to,
colours vivid in the eyes
of wetted stones,
their glosses quickly drying off.
Happiness can feel like that -
radiant then gone.

Muted wakefulness returns
but there were minutes
you felt grand - a wind-breathed tree
suddenly stood up
inside your body. Smiling,
you liked the look of your life.

Two

They take their usual places
at the table. Over supper
they talk about the day, their years

together. They are just two men
holding each other at arms length,
dancing a slow cathartic waltz.

Things shift in and out of focus
as they swirl memories around
like the wine left in their glasses.

Bestiary

Feste

You nose about the garden paths
between the peonies,
sniffing opportunities
among the tiny aftermaths
spring rains have prompted in the soil.

Your ears all angles, on alert
for rustles and stirrings,
insect wing-beats, whirrings,
as I, too, scrabble up the dirt
to bury bulbs like pirate-spoil.

You lift the ground sheet where I pot
new plants, creep in and screen
yourself under the green
plastic: a game of trying not
to be discovered, though your tail,

stuck out, betrays your hiding place.
Suddenly you shoot
off playfully and scoot
across the lawn, giving chase
to nothings as you twist and flail.

Just as suddenly you flop
on the bench. There you judge
the world safe and don't budge
again for hours. Only the sop
of supper will prompt you to mail

yourself through the cat flap, and shrink
the contents of your bowl,
mouthing a joyous howl
at what you find there. Then you wink
forty times, having found your Grail.

Tortoise

Primal-looking, scaly
crag for a head;
mouth opening a pink,
gummy, Granny grin.
And tightly packaged
like a four-legged pie
walking up to table
from the land of Cockayne.

Spreadeagled in your suit
of whorly horn,
as you breast-stroke forward,
doing your cumbersome
push-ups like a clockwork toy,
you stick your neck out
risking the unknown,
the air that might be jaws.

An ancient of days,
crawling through gardens,
zoos, sometimes centuries,
your head's beaky profile
like a can-opener
for slowly piercing
lids of low-down leaves,
their cans of fibrous juice.

Among the feet and legs
that tire and grow old
and fall away, you take
a long view, there in straw,
bedding down in boxes,
or under autumns' drifts,
steadily catching up
us short-lived, sprinting hares.

Hare

It's said you never go home straight,
but run as if you tossed a dice
inside of you from hand to hand.
Mad hackney cab, you lurch this way, now that,
shaken over the camber down your spine.

In dew-filled ruts, around green stems of wheat,
below-stairs, under trees, a cat-of-woods;
on aerodromes, a thing of flight:
you're living on the stubble of yourself,
a nibbler at the roots of things.

Secret ambassador from way out there,
always dispersing, just a smoky glimpse
of scurry and a back-door scut.
You have the trick of vanishing, a trick
long-eared ambassadors do well.

owl

sawn-off log for a heart-shaped face
with a bent nail hammered in
reclusive hunter of the lower air

Nike of Samothrace in flight
wings raised like flails to thresh life from
some shit-scared scurrying thing

grappling hook talons for undercarriage
lowered on a runway of flesh and blood
touch-down an explosion of feathers screams

plucking strings from a harp of meat
constantly feeding the rapacious beaks
of dandelion-downy chicks

crumbly pellets of fur and bone
inventory creatures
ripped and lifted out of life

reclusive so I've jig-sawed this
from books and video from film
no straight-edged piece for what's alive

Moldwarp

A blind, velvet purse
pocketing small change
among roots, insects
and mycelia.
Here's your signature -
crumbly cones of soil.

And your pink secrets
upturned on the lawn,
frozen to death. Small
Kraken from below
zero, something once
breast-stroking through earth.

There you recycled
air to breathe beneath
fastidious lawns.
Subterranean
squirrel, lardering
worms, slugs, for later.

You're a lighted fuse
burning through darkness
to these explosions
of dirt and you here,
dead, as though hoisted
with your own pétard.

More of you out there,
working in the dark
at your underground
ministries of mole -
scratching a living,
an itch in the earth.

Note: Moldwarp is a dialect term for a mole.

Swan songs

1.

In Sibelius, or Saint-Saëns,
a music sings to us of swans.
Tchaikovsky has another take
involving doubles, night, a lake;
symbolising what is hidden,
unconsciously desired, forbidden -
Rothbart's deceptive fair-ground ride,
where swans, like graceful dodgems, slide
about disturbingly as black and white
confusions of a moon-lit night.
No purchase, grip or trusted hold -
a world of slippage, ancient-old
inside of us, where pros and cons
equivocate themselves as swans.

2.

Touch-down: a comic water-ski display,
wing-fold flapping and spray;
symbolic instantly,
on lake or pond.

Take-off: running on water, then lift,
ascension, upward sift,
shaking off water, free,
away, beyond.

3.

A white embodiment of calm
floats by serenely on its glide
across a lake: cue music's balm -
as if, oboe-voiced, the swan tried
to sing our sorrow. O white psalm

of folded parchment, crystal, salt,
sliding like the tears that slalom
down our griefs - those losses that halt
us in our lives. Linen-whiteness
napkined on water, stealing the show,
in the spotlight of your brightness,
pin-drop silence falls like snow.
Expression of mute grace, of poise,
music beyond the day's white noise.

Rescue greyhounds

They are delicate Ferraris,
quietly idling on a leash.
Their springy trot is like dressage
performed on dining table legs
as elegant as Chippendale.
Their thighs, though, bulge with panniers
of muscle they've no use for now.

Pointed jaws like bicycle seats,
they're always grinning toothily,
as if unzipping their long mouths.

Gentle, contrary to myth,
they lean against you, slightly lost,
as they are reinvented now:
new names, routines and chewy toys.

Retired, they'll need a king-size bed -
think motor-bikes you keep indoors -
to snooze three quarters of each day.
Yes, Sleeping Beauty is your guest.

What do they dream of hours and hours?
It's said they're lazy, so no *Hunt by Night*,
no wood they're threading shuttle-fast,
stretched out like swimmers in a race.

Along with lions, he-goats, kings,
the Bible names them one of four
things that are 'comely in going'.
Owners, lovingly besotted,
would readily agree with this,
although the 'kings' make me doubt
they're necessarily so.

Whale

Beneath sea-storms -
hurricanoes' cracking cheeks -
huge substance
brushes through dark rooms,
blue on blue. Gliding tonnage,
like a cliff sliding past,
swimming round
the planet's bowl.

Vast movers, solemn
hoovers of the deeps'
enormous swarms of krill;
sucking squillions in -
boat-sized, ladled scoops
of fish soup warming
in a sea-wide tureen.

How they croon, putter,
chunt, bubble and squeak
like tuning radios,
humungous baby-talk,
sea-searching echoes.

High-jumping out of water,
they swoon
like dynamited chimneys
and, falling, pound waves
playing knock-knock
on the ocean's door.

Their skeletons
are beautiful, vaulted naves.
Giant secateurs
for jaw-bones,
white tunnels of ribs, staves
picked clean of blubber, song.
War graves.

Pilgrim

In the middle of its back
it balances a round home;
all its goods in a ruck-sack
like an enamelled dome,

or one of those shaped casings
- hiding a running-board wheel -
with bossed, metal facings
on a Thirties coupe de ville.

It does not think, has no mind
to twist the Möbius strip
of self-awareness. It's a kind
of slipper giving the slip.

It has no roots, staying put
is not on its agenda.
It floats on its non-stick foot
elongated to slender

suction pad. It has no shoes
to put on, no toes are curled,
no sat-nav sibyl, no muse,
just tenderness tightly furled.

Not much forgiveness for this
pilgrim resting under logs
and pots, in damp cavities
and watering-cans it clogs.

Mercy perhaps feels like rain
dropping on the garden path,
an impromptu gushing drain
giving it both drink and bath.

Yet it survives somehow, slides,
shrinks, taking time out - a brief spell
from pilgrimage - while it hides
in the cockle of its shell.

Inky

Chunky black comma when asleep -
to show he's pausing
for a game of playing dead
until there's food. Ammonite-curled,
he circles silence, one of many
he keeps warm each day.

Comatose sun-worshipper
prostrated on a sunlit floor,
rolling over like a toppled pawn
into adjacent squares of shine,
paws held limply on his chest
as if too lazy to sit up and beg.

Pear-shaped bollard,
reserving a place for the sun to park
on the morning path,
he sniffs the air's pomander
copiously cloved with breathing news
he seems indifferent to, closing his eyes.

Soft cushions for his pummelling
or samplers for his needlepoint,
all laps are WELCOME doormats for his knead.
Not able to count seven yet,
he wreathes him only two or three times round,
elegantly docking nose to tail.
A bubbly humming simmers in his throat.

Lullaby for Feste

Rest now, the lamp's
white sun shines over
your sleepy head,
keeping you warm
at the edge of the bed.
You'll be safe from harm -
wind-chills, grassy damps -
under the duvet-cover.

Your stomach's full,
good things in its bowl.
Your cat-nip mouse
has breathed his last
squeal and the house
prepares to fast
on a teáspoonful
of self-control.

Let the day go,
arthritic puss;
let the night wind lull
you to sleep - that dark
inside, that hull
bound like an ark,
saved for tomorrow.
Hush, shsh-shsh, süss...

Elegies

Little Elegies

1.

A picture of a caravan,
camels seen from the air
as they snake their way along dunes;
like hopes threading a needle's eye
to an imagined paradise.

The sands seem ridged with finger prints.
Deep hollows in them look like caves,
resemble intimate places
on a body, groins the wind
has sculpted with its tongue.

Riderless camel caravan:
newly-departed souls set out,
unable to let desire go.
One man is leading them. Ahead
a desert's dessicated waves.

Brown camels - with blue blankets
spread out as saddles over them -
walking in file, scooping the sand.
Through their ox-bows they meander,
sedately shuffling to Ophir.

2.

Each day at his desk, little came;
a few themes on slips of paper -
brief telegrams from a desert place -
all juice, all life gone underground.

Surrounding him, as dense as fog,
depression closed in, cut him off;
began the years that ruined, drained
him to the bottom of a glass.

The nights were hard, much too quiet,
too like the clearing in his head
where he waited less hopefully
each day, longing for it to end.

Years falling short of promise -
a fresh-air, early billowing
that proved ephemeral. Hardest
of all, the looks in colleagues' eyes.

3.
Oval, oxidised-green, bronze greaves -
loot from some ancient battlefield -
looking like frost-damaged leaves
fallen too soon. Three of hundreds
stripped from warm shins.

Backbones are thimble-pitted stones.
Lodged between vertebrae, the head
of an arrow. They might be bones
from a dried up *osso bucco*
but for the bronze.

Feet skeletons. In the right one
an arrow through the tarsal bones,
only half scraped free from the dun,
compacted earth that buried them.
An old man's feet.

Gruesome discoveries, remains
lifted from their obscurities
under baked crusts of hilltops, plains,
where once the day was pitiless,
now pitiful.

Fayum portraits

The dead keep on surprising us,
all dressed up in the dark
like party guests waiting for their host.

From coffin-boards and mummy-cloths,
looking out to see who's there,
they stare at us, full-face.

Their portraits show them young again,
their finery and coiffured hair,
with eyes wide-open, olive-dark,

almost confrontational,
as if they look us up and down,
astonished to find us in their way.

Some eyes betray a tenderness
as though recalling distant violence.
A child frowns as if puzzled by death.

They seem brimful, about to spill
confidences, what their lives tasted like,
but keep their distance as they stare

like passengers, looking out of windows
on a train halted here.
I think they are pitying us

and saddened we're still weathered by the air,
its heat and winds they have done with.
They can't remember what it's like

to change, although they are wrapped up
pupae-snug and already changed.
They smell of dust and interrupted dreams.

Note: Fayum portraits are mummy portraits dating from 1st century BC,
found in the Fayum basin near Cairo.

Ghosting
(i.m. J.T.)

1.

What you planted comes back
as fingerprints you left
in tulip, daffodil,
anemone de Caen.
The garden doesn't know
its gardener has died.

Books emptied from your shelves,
are stacked in boxes now
as if you moved elsewhere
and left me here to pack
without a new address
to send them on to you.

I try to imagine you
as absent, gone abroad,
dream of you coming back,
descending from a train,
arms held out to hug me.
And my heart, my heart lifts.

2.

Friends can't believe you're dead.
So much alive in them
they feel you like a pulse,
hear your voice when they read
your books, watch videos
conjure you out of air.

Small objects open doors
to hauntings joyous-sad.
Momentarily, you
return, like all those bulbs
you planted year on year
now lighting up the earth.

How radioactive
love is, energies left
behind to work in us,
their half-lives like ticking
in a car's bodywork,
its journey cooling down.

We are just clerks of grief,
sad ghost-writers, raking
the embers, kindling
an afterlife for you.
Who are you becoming?
What will your voice sound like?

Bookmark
(i.m. T.D.)

From gawky boyhood
to the middle of his life,
six photos - of a poet
who died too soon - printed
each side of a bookmark,
touchingly tipped into
his final collection.

Like a speeded-up film
his life fast-forwards,
showing how his clothes change
from flares to formal suit
and looks change, too; his hair
receding more and more
while his smile gets broader.

He ages in seconds:
now a tight-lipped boy,
now grinning young man,
now beaming, middle-aged.
More at home in himself?
The bookmark's like a dash
between the dates of his life.

I studied it for a while
then put it between the leaves
of his book, surrounded
by his final poems,
as if burying him
in his own longship
with all his goods about him.

One photo periscopes
from the pages - that shy boy.
He looks like a stowaway
who knows the great journey
he's hoped for is ending
too soon, somehow knew
it could never be enough.

Couple

(i.m. B.B. & P.P.)

They had their own lives, cared
for each others', visited
as sunlit or rainy weather;
and they made one together,
like gin and tonic
happily paired.

How to balance, stand
alone and lean against?
How to be themselves;
and, all the while, two halves:
to be partners each side
of their ampersand?

Often they waited outside
each other, separate,
absent, would commiserate
in letters. Love, like a great
sea-swell, buoyed them, floated them
out on its tide.

❋

Sea-shimmer, and a hushing
music from reed-beds,
and churned shingle like chains
loosened underfoot, and rains
freshing the beach
waves keep rushing.

Poised, above a strong,
high wind's keening
monotony, a voice
rises over sharp annoys
shifting in the undertow,
cradles its song

like a drifting boat
and cries alone. A buoy,
tolling of danger beneath,
says the heart has teeth
and for its bite
there is no antidote.

"O, my America"
(i.m. Thom Gunn)

1.
Sad captain, now you shine
among the crew of stars
you made a firmament:
habitués of bars
and baths with whom you spent
good, anonymous times
dissolving 'yours' and 'mine'.

You wanted to uncurb
yourself, were determined
to speed through life. Licence
was something to drive the mind,
not quite an innocence,
more delight in being
an irregular verb

that did not conjugate
like others. You thought skin
another consciousness
you could be happy in
and found your own undress
a state you had to learn
as if a neonate.

2.
You loved your house on Cole,
liked gardening, cats and cooking
(though you weren't very good).
And you valued the whole
house eating home-cooked food,
sharing news of good-looking

guys, writer's block, the neighbourhood
gossip, and AIDs taking its toll.

One house-mate proudly said
to the paramedic who came
"This is the poet Thom Gunn,"
as if he introduced
you, mortal on your bed.
As if you must get used
to others saying what you'd done,
who you were, using your name,
lying there like a page - bemused
faces over you - being read.

Elsewheres

Nature Reserve

High water levels
sop at paths among willow,
witchhazel and sedge.

Painted route-markers
on the narrows winding through
flooded quarry-pits,

lead us to bird-hides
and wide viewpoints. A swan sleeps
on its reflection,

on a white pillow:
emblem of what we yearn for -
to float for a while.

Half a mile away,
train clatter and quarry-dredge
border the reserve.

Mothers push buggies
heavy with their tomorrows.
Toddlers take their time

and the swan does, too;
seemingly serene, folded
into its own wings.

Runners anxiously
check how much time has elapsed,
how much they have left,

glancing at watches
on their wrists like manacles,
as if on the run.

On the canal

At locks, such busyness -
winding sluices, toeing
gates open; happiness,
a lock-stair left behind.
Then it's easy-going
miles, opening their door
to somewhere in your mind
you know you came here for.

The anglers' listless floats,
two cygnets and a swan,
ducks, painted narrow-boats,
the canal's regulars,
their traffic going on
alongside bungalows,
brisk dog-walkers, parked cars,
and statuesque willows.

Here the long sleeve of care
you've knitted unravels
on this slow thoroughfare
of tow-paths and lock-gates;
of leisurely travels
where an altogether
other state of mind waits
with its own kind weather.

You're afloat and your thoughts,
between the fore and aft
of the boat, circle noughts
and add them to your sum
of happiness: your craft
in motion with the stream
of your mind, as in some
long, satisfying dream.

On a channel that floats
along dug corridors
past other narrow-boats
and backs of warehouses,
time becomes re-wind, pause,
slow-motion, quiet drift.
Anxiety drowses.
Let it go, let it sift.

Swona

like a table-top in the sea.
Descendants of a herd of cows

left behind forty years ago
have gone wild and graze it now.

They have forgotten humankind
were ever here. A huge, white one,

thickly quilted with muscle, frowns
and frowns at us and doesn't blink.

We are unwanted, keep our distance,
redundant in their world of sea-

surrounded grass, where they stand still,
waiting for us who don't belong

to vanish soon as if we're ghosts.
They never really needed us.

Light seems to wipe the island clean.
It can barely say 'Once...' to us.

Between

Interstices, mortar in gaps,
those commas when you lean
on breath and turn, adjust; perhaps
emptying the washing machine,
or cleaning out the litter-tray,
that in-between,
putting the cutlery away.

The whispers of a shifting house,
the squeaks and murmurs of its cage
of wood and plumbing, like a mouse
pittering away there backstage,
whilst you intently listen to
its slow suffrage,
barely conscious of what you do.

Those odd few seconds when you're not
quite focussed on the job as planned,
you're a contingent astronaut
voyaging somewhere near at hand -
the tumble dryer's rounding drone,
white-noises, bland
as refrigerators switching on.

Those shifts, transitions, crossings, thin
moments of blank "Now, where was I?",
these slips of reverie you're in
and out in the wink of an eye,
could they be supple cartilage
so that the I
can bend, if not rattle, its cage?

No one's at home but going on
you feel those other selves, your moons,
distending you. Their orbits' wan
attractions pause your afternoons
in reverie at desk or sink,
washing the spoons:
you blink much larger than you think.

Liminal

A sticky fingered ghost?
Persuade yourself it's just

a web collecting dust,
not some invisible thing

clinging to your hand or substance
thinly trickling through the dark.

Traces of flour on a chair,
a dusting on a wall,

tell-tale signs of moonlighting,
a pop-up in your breakfast room,

as if night-bakers loafed here
on a break from earning

crusts they make, watching
dough breathing babyly?

Going to raid the fridge,
a shudder of cold air

swipes you on the stairs.
Something is stealing your heat

in the origami rooms
moonlight folds indoors.

Stair-creak and curtain lift,
calling cards small as the hours,

evidences enough,
taking you for a ride,

then doubted, come daylight's
plausible grey fingerprints.

Yes, say they're just a trick,
no first-footings elsewhere.

Fishing in Tomis

That man fishing, right at the end
of his tether, out on the pier,
still hopes that Augustus will send
for him, make Tomis disappear
like a nightmare he's had. Years now
he's been angling for forgiveness.

Where the pier points an accusing
finger at the sea, all he's lost
wallows there like a whale confusing
itself in the shallows. Tossed
by wave on wave, his grief's too big
to sink or find a way back out.

Tomis is just a parapet
where past and future sheer away,
leaving him the present, its regret
of having nothing else to say,
save that he longs to be in Rome
or in his thinning dreams of it.

His *tristia*, like an oil-spill,
makes rainbows of his misery
as he dips, dips his angling quill
in the ink-well of the Black Sea.
In this cul-de-sac at the world's end,
each line he casts hooks his own mouth.

Life-changing loss: just where he is
becomes as far as he can get
in this life. Exiled at Tomis,
perhaps he owes Caesar a debt?
Pushed out to the edge of his world,
fishing from the brim of himself,

he gets to look over the rim
and instead of the nothingness
he supposed there, could see for him-
self the Rome he worships is less
than he imagines. If, of course,
he has the courage to look down.

Escape

Boat-bow furl, the little ruck of it,
purling over - silk disturbed, slight
gatherings and smoothings out

of water pushed aside beneath
your passage through reflected trees,
immobile clouds, trailing a hand.

The quiet of your blood to listen to,
the heart's faithful service below-deck,
leisurely progress through canals.

Sunshine slicks a warm patina
over you; motion purrs, it breathes
like gossamer against your face.

Let there be nothing else but this,
a long, blue corridor of sky.

BETWEEN THE TWO OF US

Shipwrecked

Blinking, you are washed up at last.

After months of swimming, you have finally reached dry land.

You unfurl your old man's fingers, wrinkled from the wet.

The plates inside your head edge still closer, like prim sweethearts.

Already, explorers are laying claim to parts of this newly-discovered
continent:

His father's eyes. His mother's nose. Your ears, a distant cousin,
newly dead.

Once you have realised the stubborn ribs have gone, you will stretch
out,

uncurling like a fern-frond in some timeless forest.

One day too, you will stand on a tidal beach

and stare at the sea for the very first time

and feel that you have returned

to somewhere you once called home.

Newborn

What looks like tissue wraps you up;
your head a little berry, oval-shaped,
cocooned in sheets and blanket wool.

On dry land but not ready yet
to give up floating, here you are,
seriously sleeping after birth.

Your parents are saying your name,
practising it to welcome you.
Wake up soon, hear what love sounds like.

Man and Boy

I wanted to plant six, one for each year.
You said nine was your favourite number.

I said each bulb was a little miracle.
You told me that only Jesus could perform those.

I thought each green tip was a hand shooting up in class.
You said they were rockets blasting off to the moon.

I ransacked colour charts to describe the blue.
You said we had a pot full of sky.

I felt they were as sad as spent fireworks.
You told me meteorites didn't last long either.

I stood there thinking this was a metaphor.
You went off to find something better to do.

Meeting

"Don't talk to strange men", mother said.
Ironic, that I've gone to bed
with strange men, stayed with one for life.

Meeting who I was when a boy,
what might we possibly say
to each other, past and future?

No. There'd be no conversation,
not even a hesitation.
No exception to a mother's rule

for him yet - too young, much too shy -
but true to his Don'ts, walking by
oblivious, his mother's son

for a little longer, with me
looking at his ship all at sea
in a bottle about to smash.

A Mother's Love

Picture a series of photographs.

The garden stays the same in all of them,
a child's dressing-up box of colours.
Plants plonked where there is room.
Here, like Barnardo's, none is turned away,
all are given a chance.

In the background, the gardener.
At first, she stands stiff and proud,
eye-balling the camera, defying it to lie.
Perhaps, she is thinking that's how photographers
tell brides to stand. Perhaps.
She is the one who never married.

But frame by gentler frame she relaxes
until one protective arm uncoils itself
along the top of a fence and
she gazes, not at the lens, but out,
out across her garden,
staring with a mother's love, unconditional and permanent.

Naturally, she blames herself when flowers fail:
too much light, too little water.
Each empty space a stab to the heart,
each shrivelled stem a death wound.
Handing herself in to the police, she pleads guilty
to letting them down and signs her confession with a flourish.
Yet how she rejoices as each happy accident
buds, swells and bursts open, refusing to accept any credit.
Her flowers her teeming family,
the wayward and the reliable, the unruly and the quiet.

All are noticed, all proudly pointed out,
all are valued, cherished, loved.
When she thinks nobody is there,
she whispers, "I love you."
Yet not one replies, "And I love you too!"
Not one. Not one. Not one.

In the garden

In her wayward garden serpents are avoided.
Postponing wilderness again, she finds
the vigour of her plants surprises her
while her neglect of them no longer does.

Children leave her to the dying light,
indulgent if the lawn is playable.
The friend her husband has become
paroles her until tea-time
puppets both to show their crumpled love.

She stands out there suburban Eve,
gardening a small way back to Eden
yet a little forward to Jerusalem,
using the intensity of spadework
to secure a holiday from being timed
and ticked-off by her clocks -
her sense that she stands in the swathe
of their relentless, scything hands.

Not subject to the hour but the season,
such temporal afflictions
as a house and husbandry evaded,
she lets go of the familiar, pulling hands
choosing for herself this occupation.

She will come in reluctantly aware
of having made the umpteenth start
on her oasis where she walks among
the green, neglected gestures of her heart.

Viking, North Utsire

She is the first one to arrive because she always is.
He will arrive five minutes later
As punctual as the shipping forecast.

Checking her face in the driving mirror:
non-committal, guarded, ageing,
her desperation - or is it boredom? -
lies buried deep, weighted down,
an inconvenient corpse.

By now the sex is as routine as door to door inquiries
and as predictable as the tides.

She pulls hard on her cigarette
- As luck would have it his wife smokes too! -
And forces herself to concentrate on
The ways the breeze moves through the branches.
Mindfulness.Her therapist's trick.

Next, a teenager again, she chews a stick of pink bubble gum,
Which will lose its flavour just as he draws up.

Later he will ask her
"Why didn't we meet ten years ago?" adding
"I only stay for the kids, you know that" -
The Tyne, Dogger, Fisher of infidelity.

Tonight, though, the general synopsis seems set fair,
No attention all shipping, no warning of gales.
Yet, as he speaks, she finds herself
Responding to the rise and fall of his voice
Like a trawler rides the swell in Viking or North Utsire,
Not listening to the words, realising that lies
Are much more reassuring than the truth
Provided you don't believe in them.

Seasons

When you don't feel sexy-
looking in your lover's eyes,
and you close the bedroom door,
hiding away your nudity
like a rhetoric that doesn't work,
what is it you feel then?

Loss and sadness? Maybe
less obvious, a feeling of relief
those accidents of surface, shapes,
can matter less, you might be seen
beneath whatever spell of his
had cast its bright net over you?

As if you have a secret name
he could, at last, decipher like a rune;
or you can say your own now differently,
and talk about the things you two have lost -
looks, hopes and dreams, persona worn
for years and then outgrown.

You might now see a mundane grace
exists between the two of you
whatever change there is -
that simply loves the seasons of your life,
autumn's undress most beautiful of all,
when ripe and ruin walk there hand in hand.

The Figure on the Edge

The guide book tells me it's a teaching window -
designed for those who think words are for thinking and saying,
rather than reading - a lesson for the eyes.

This is a familiar scene: a god-fearing father,
his knife whetted and poised,
calm as if about to carve the Sunday roast;
a ram, forever trapped and struggling;
a son compliant, desperate to please;
an angelic intervention in the nick of time.

Yet it is the colours which have the power to amaze:
the hilltops as purple as a maturing bruise;
that cloak, ripe blackberries; that sliding river, a peacock's breast;
that globe of fire, a golden, burning sunset.
All produced by craftsmen, nameless and unknown,
as anonymous as a poison-pen letter.

I spot him, almost as an afterthought, the figure on the edge,
about to slip out of sight. Unnoticed, unremarkable.
His clothes, red as spilt blood, his hair a dab of English mustard.
Yet he looks not in wonder at this hilltop scene, nor idle curiosity,
rather as if it was not at all significant,
at least not for such a one as him, a figure on the edge.
Perhaps he has a latch to mend, a roof waiting to be fixed.
So many better things to do than stand about, impatient to be off.
His donkey, grey as old age, ears pricked, is aware something is not
    quite right.

A teaching window, true enough, but just what lesson here is being
    taught?

Annunciation

(Sandro Botticelli)

He says 'Hail Mary'. As if touched, she shies
away like a leaf flustered by the breeze
his wing-flutter stirs in the Renaissance room.

And all the apparatuses are there -
the swan-like angel wings, a chequered floor
and him, posed genuflecting at her feet.

His draperies are inflating balloons
of red silk. The slant stem of the lily,
held like a pen, seems nibbed to write his news.

The lily-bling, the silks, the wings, are meant
to press into her heart, as if she's wax;
her body an envelope for the child.

That gesture when she moves away from him
as though she is contagious now - her life
a petri dish, the good news spreading there.

The Cup of Tea
(Mary Cassatt 1880)

First of all, the cup, of course.
Centred, white bone china, wedding-ringed,
the kind a clumsy aunt will drop and wreck the set.

A blue chair, as comforting as morphine,
waiting for its chance to become shabby chic.

Behind, a tub shaped like a baby's coffin
where a jungle of blooms jostle for attention,
one already on the turn.

Her arm, encased in a long, ivory glove
like a plaster cast, throbs and aches
but putting it down will spoil her sister's painting.

Her dress, tangerine with slashes
of anaemic pink, like a patient's gown
after a botched operation.

That slight swelling of her stomach
is not a sign that she is with child
or has over-indulged on fondant dainties.
Rather it hints at the medical something
with the unpronounceable name
that will shortly kill her.

So she gazes out, not at
guests with their fluting chit-chat
but at something else entirely.
She has already gone from here.

Yet when for the very first time
she looks at her portrait,
completed, finished, done,
she has never, ever, felt more alive.

On a Balcony
(Mary Cassat, 1878-9)

Lydia has folded the newspaper
to a whitened pane of glass.
Tiny newsprint, like see-through holes,
provides a window with a view.

Her dress is printed too, a white
billowy muslin like a cloud
of unreadable history,
the apparent muteness of a swan.

Behind her a trough of flowers
understudies her brief flourishing
in the fifth act of her life.

If we could hear it, something sings
quietly - a solo cello
in the orchestra of herself.

Pushing Up the Snowdrops
(i. m. Glyn Smith)

In Russia they call
corpses - emerging from deep-freeze
as the winter snow slowly melts away - snowdrops.
The drunkard for whom one for the road
was an easy mistake to make.
The wife whose Christmas present
was one punch too many.
But this is not Russia.

Once I knew a galanthophile.
Whose only fetish was
a passion for snowdrops.

All of those dainty drop-pearls
looked the same to me
but he was a sharp-eyed teacher
faced with a fresh September class
or a farmer naming each and every cow.
He knew his snowdrops.

He'd drool over bulb catalogues
at Galanthus Green Tear
or sigh with unrequited love
at Galanthus Elizabeth Howard, the only other woman
he was ever tempted by.

Once he speculated heavily
on Galanthus Ikariae, which staying hidden,
covered up like the perfect crime,
broke his heart, big as it was.

Far too early it was his turn to be covered up,
his coffin splashing into a waterlogged hole
as if we were burying him at sea.
No chance of him reappearing.
Instead, seeing these optimistic flowers
peeking through, I like to think
he's giving the first ones
a gentle push, encouraging
them to suss out the place before
that heave, spilling out the rest,
spreading like a juicy rumour.

"They'll clump up, given time," he'd told me
and as usual he'd been exactly right.

Snowdrops

(for Dave)

Drifts of white nodding
stooped over shivering grass,

like tired magi at oases
on their journeys home.

From earth's frosted crumble
beside our bootsoles,

clustered like footprints
lightly filled with snow,

they light the way to Spring,
tiny lanterns held aloft.

A Simple Sign

It has seen better days, no doubt.
Once, though, that tarnished plaque
would have sparkled like innocence.

Is this where you'd saunter along
in that slow, complacent way all lovers have?

Alone now, did you pause, like blind Gloucester,
on this cliff edge and dare yourself to jump?
Maybe you held back, fearful
you'd be falling through all eternity.
Love, not conscience, makes cowards of us all.

Or rather did you test the post for firmness
and, a little out of breath from all that exertion,
walk briskly away, tools in hand,
a blister already forming, thinking about a job well-done?

Is your love still comfortable,
like singing along to the car radio?
Or do the years, like the waves, fret and chafe,
a swelling tumour gnawing at your insides?

One day, soon, the sea will lose all patience with the land
and your simple sign will slurry down the slope.

Returning, you'll only see what isn't there.

Blue Gate

(after Winifred Nicholson)

A blue, barred gate, thin fencing either side,
a scrap of threshold, one world to another,
with views of sea, and islands and beyond.

Just push against its wooden ribs and go.
Your heart could lift as if an angel stood
beside each doorway in a fall of sun.

The gate has lost its catch and idly swings,
as you do, open and shut, watching how
it offers such largesse then takes it back

like two minds you are in between -
yearning for sunset's changeable, red rose
while living by the clock's blushed face.

Likely all of us will meet a blue gate
once, choosing to go through it or to stay,
only later on find how it changed us:

what kites flew in us or collapsed back then,
how thankfully, regretfully - how will we know? -
we seem to have been living ever since.

Captured on Film

She was not going to risk missing it.
A sight to lock safely away, like trapping
the taste of black market coffee
in the throat, long after that last, slow sip
has completely drained your cup.

The bride, her bouquet as big as a lifebelt.
The black and white groom, posing for a photo-shoot
like a Hollywood star emerging from a screening.

Somebody calls her back inside but she pauses
to watch a sleek getaway car speed past,
allowing them to escape to their future together,
leaving her to imagine the day
she will stop being just plain Anne Frank
and become Mrs Somebody Else instead.

TRY A TRIP ON ROUTE 160 TO REIGATE - DAILY FROM STOCKWELL STATION

the homeward way
in the cool of the day
- London Transport poster by Walter Spradbery, 1914

Mid-distance, up the hill,
a bus diminishes
along a bowling-smooth,
green road. An embering
horizon lights it home.

A stair-well skelters down
the back, the lower deck
glows with light. On top,
skittled with silhouettes,
is open to the air.

The suburb's quiet dusk
is cool as calamine
against the brimful cheeks
of ripe, day-out faces
holding their trip unspilt.

The bus, like a candle,
lights a darkening world.
Sleepy trippers going home
to beds in Stockwell,
maybe Reigate in their dreams.

A few more rides at dusk,
the moon peeking through trees
like a hide-and-seek child.
A few more comings home
safely after days out.

DAVE SMITH

For Jane. For everything.

To Katherine, Sarah and Tom.

Swiss Army Poem

Here, let me show you.
This one captures the messy taste of watermelon.
Look. This one tickles like your giddy first kiss.
See, this one jemmies the box where you had hidden your secrets.
This funny little one? I have absolutely no idea.
Perhaps it's just to put a smile on your face.
Please be careful how you close them though;
These things are sharp, your skin so unprotected.

Tick Tock

I don't believe in clocks,
being jealous of their faultless rhythm.
I have not measured out my life in coffee spoons
nor listened out for time's winged chariot,
yet I still stand. Just.
Like a groggy boxer or a struggling teacher,
hanging on in there for the bell.
There goes a second. And another one.
And another.

The Safe Side

Most miss the hut on their dash to the dunes.
its felt roof peeling like sun-burnt skin.

Once a builder tried to convince me its woodworm
was down to an ill-placed dartboard then
prised a price from out of his toolbox.

For a second, sex on the beach was more than a drink
Shabby chic at the seaside Shangri-la Brigadoon
before being swept out on a rip-tide
of Friday night hold-ups, coastal erosion,
even floating away like Noah on his flood.

Now, walking the shoreline, seals on sentry duty,
I'm skinny dipping by starlight, spitting out saltwater,
but keeping to the narrow concrete path,
straight ahead, just to be on the safe side.

Ways Of Seeing

I notice a patch of damp requiring attention.
She sees the arc of a rainbow.

For me, they are a rich source of vitamin C.
For her, shiny, dangling marbles. A festival of blackcurrants.

I fear the storm clouds threatening a downpour.
She wants somebody to turn the Sun back on.

I know the bulb of the reading lamp needs replacing.
She strokes its long, long neck, like a giraffe's.

I stand there useless, powerless to help.
She sees Mummy's eyes are leaking, finds a tissue to fix them.

Now, as she stands on tippy-toe and stares hard at me,
I keep asking myself, just what can she see?

In Passing

Speccy Harris said I'd walk the 11+.
Every week on Mrs Carrington's classroom wall
my ever-expanding galaxy of bright red stars
totally eclipsed his measly constellation.
If it had been a prep school
rather than just Spring Street Juniors
he would have been labelled a plodder,
a bit of a duffer. Almost a dunce.

So it was some surprise that morning
to find him on our front doorstep,
breathless, after what passed for sprinting,
waving his letter around like a wallet
he was about to hand in,
confident of a generous reward.

Our doormat was as empty as a politician's promises.

No blazer then for me, with its Latin crest.
No school tie, stripes in house colours.
No leather satchel. No rugby boots.
Instead jeans and Brylcreemed hair.
A sly fag at breaktime, then
pretending the cane didn't hurt that much.

I had been stopped at the border,
accused of not having the right papers.
My past was behind me but so was my future.
Until, that is, our letter box rattled
and my passport dropped to the floor.
Speccy had forgotten to mention
that the postman was on his way.

"I knew we'd pass," he said
in the playground before heading off
to torment Dennis Dale and Michael Page.
Two of life's failures, just turned eleven.

We'd passed. Fair enough.
Some people are scared of clowns
but my worst nightmares feature
a postman walking past our house.

Coming Of Age

Mum took me to help choose the pram,
Dad having said that his job was done.
"Remember, we're not made of money," she mouthed,
a nervous ventriloquist just starting out.
Our choice in the end looked sufficiently posh.
Chrome as shiny as Judas's silver.
A hand-painted rose, perpetually in bloom.
Mum's growing-up boy counted the cash,
fresh from hibernating in the tin near the telly.
Now the assistant, hushed and efficient,
like a funeral director preparing a body.
"We refund, of course. If anything goes wrong."
The trapdoor springs open.
I dangle, a man.

Sir Had Said

Miss had said, "If the whole class was a set of dominoes
You'd be the double blank." She was right.
Teachers talked to me in crossword clues;
Only Sir from Rural Science talked any sense. Miss had said,
"Poetry is words that send a shiver right along your brain."
Well, Sir was my Shakespeare then. He breathed Romance
And instant coffee: "Fresian. Brahman. The Galloway Beltie.
Charolais. Limousin. The Blonde d'Aquitaine."

The prize for Rural Science was the only thing I'd ever won.
I imagined a brand new spade, hefting it for balance and for weight.
A D-shaped handle, a shaft of polished ash, a heart-shaped blade.
Spear-sharp, it would slice through soil as I, slowly, effortlessly,
Rhythmically, turned over row after row after row.
"Don't be daft," Sir had said, "Can't see the Chair of Governors with
    a spade!
It has to be a book." He sighed. "Try to choose one that might be of
    some use."

I stood outside the bookshop as if it was a mosque.
Inside, I saw him straightaway, stooped over, a breaktime fagger.
Sir was looking like a top set kid, ogling a maths exam.
I waited until he'd slipped the book back, lovingly, into place.

Next day at school, I handed him the title: "The Joy of Sex."
"I doubt it," Sir had said, "But I will try my best."
At that awkward ceremony, the Chair of Governors gave me
"The Joys of Gardening" and I gave it to my Mum, unopened and
    unread.
She'd take down exhibit A for visitors as proof her lad was not so
    daft at all.
"Top of the class!" she'd say; "Out of twelve," I'd mumble to the
    floor.

About that time, Yvonne let me think I'd taken her to the woods.
I kissed her cheek as a sparrow pecks at crumbs.
"I'm not your auntie," she had said before her eager
And experienced lips sucked all the breath from me.
"And I bet you think your willy's just for peeing out of."
She was right. I did....But not for that much longer.
Yvonne had conjurer's fingers and me, the wide-eyed volunteer,
Prepared to be baffled and amazed, was sawn in half.

That summer, I wrote a book inside my head, with chapters
Called Valerie and Angela, Jacqueline and Sue.
And Sir had said, "Some folks don't need books, they learn by
    doing."

Binoculars

When I take out Dad's binoculars
I can always smell the hope.
The final time (although neither of us knew that it would be the last)
he tried to spur my interest in the sport of kings
I told him he was flogging a dead horse instead of backing it.
It was the kind of comment I thought was smart.
I knew he would abandon me like a January puppy
to find the wink, the nudge in the right direction,
the tip, the sly word if not from the horse's mouth,
well, straight from the stable lad's at least.
Once found, I'd be urged to lump on, to splash the cash
and as usual I'd smugly refuse,
scared that saying yes would be a sign
that I was slowly turning into him.
Later, he counted out his winnings, note by grinning note
and tried to give me half.
So now when the twitcher behind me says that
the difference between the common snipe and Jack
is that, if I look closely, one or the other has a darker head,
all I can hear is Dad telling me to watch
our jockey in his black and white checks and quartered cap
as he eases his way to the front. You beauty!

Dad Jokes

I say. I say. I say.
I wasn't very close to Dad when he died.
A good job since he was blown up clearing a minefield.

I say. I say.
I want to go quietly in my sleep like Dad did.
Not screaming with terror like his passengers.

I say.
Dad spent a lot of money on sick animals.
He just didn't know they were sick when he backed them.

Looking back and looking up from my maths homework,
I see Dad wrestling with a problem of his own.
His text book, the folded racing page of the Daily Mirror.
Take a horse. Add in its last five outings.
Factor in the going good-to-firm. Balance probabilities.
Calculate the odds before arriving at a solution. Q.E.D.
Then off on his errand, crossing his fingers all the way.
For years I thought that bookies was slang for the library.

Now it's my turn to cross my fingers.
Which makes writing tricky.

I said.

Daddy's Little Princess

Catalogue-cute from her patent-leather shoes
to the shocking pink ribbon in her hair.
She'd much to tell him, how she could count right up to twenty
and almost write her own name, but her babbling
was drowned by a sea of hugs. She didn't even notice
Mummy waiting patiently for her turn but when it came
she tugged at her mother's dress
as if trying to part two fighting animals.
Later she will ask why Daddy can't come home with them,
leaving me to wonder just what he'd done to be inside for.

Inside Out

Step a little nearer please. Watch closely.

First, a forensic examination of the grain
whorled like dusted fingerprints. Next, plank
after plank is set aside, until one remains, unaware.
I have a grip - I'm known for it in here -
yet even I am jealous of that vice's relentless squeeze.
The plane, placid, tamed, bores me. Once set,
The only trick is knowing when to stop
and where's the skill in that? But chiselling!
Chiselling is all about control. The gentlest tickle
and a sliver furls back upon itself. See.
A change of angle and the block cracks and splits
as satisfying as any jaw or ribcage.

In the complacent, cack-handed early days,
my chisel juddered and bumped and skidded
before finding flesh as weak as pity and quickly after, bone.
I heard the laughs, I saw the smiles.
Once that would have been enough to release the beast;
a lunge, a scuffle, a scar for life, hopefully an eye.
Now it sits obediently by my side, relaxed yet ready.
This place has taught me patience if nothing else.

You are now free to leave.

Little Green Apples

Every autumn the windfall apples cobble the lawn.
Soon the cows will appear, tugged by sharp scent
and stronger instinct. Like gawpers at a car crash,
they jostle for position but quickly most decide
there's nothing much to see. A slow-moving goods train,
they stretch out in an orderly row across the field.
This year, though, one uncouples herself and pushes a photogenic head
still further through the hawthorn hedge and waits, stock still,
as if posing for her portrait, framed by a crown of thorns.
She stands as solid and as square as authority.
Her eyes, placid and unblinking, focus on the fallen crop.
Her gaze becomes a stare, her stare an obsession.
With her bulk, she could easily push her way through,
a drunken gate-crasher wreaking havoc on our newly-planted beds
yet, instead, she chooses to wait, politely, for me to intervene.
And me? I choose to carry on pegging out the washing,
cursing all duvet covers and pretending to ignore her.
But I do notice how gently she moves her pale, pink lips
in anticipation of her spittle dribbling down in one long, elastic line.
I, too, have instincts and my instinct is to feed her
but I know, unlike Eve, the danger lurking in one small apple.
So temptation must be resisted. The apples must remain untouched.
In the end, of course, she abandons her patient vigil and
with a quiet dignity, submits to the calling of the herd.
Do cattle feel disappointment? I doubt it... But they might.
So, under cover of darkness, like a sapper in the trenches,
I slip outside and lob green grenades far into no-man's-land,
listening for the soft thud as they land and roll and stop,
hoping that tomorrow she is the one to find them.

A Modern Fairytale

Once a young woman found herself boarding a bus.
She had no clear recollection of queuing up
Nor any idea where it was going, but the push
Of passengers sent her forwards and she knew better
Than to distract the driver whilst the vehicle was in motion.
Seats were few and far between but eventually one was found
And for a time she gazed out of the window as
Dog walkers stooped with their little plastic bags
And a toddler dropped his toy. Streets became fields and then streets
again.
Any questions about the bus's destination were met
With shrugs, with bemused expressions or worst, wry grins.
Occasionally someone would sit next to her:
The garrulous, the dull, the hard of hearing.
Once she had to pretend that she was Dutch
With little command of English:"No please. I was raining."
Sometimes she read to pass the time. She tried
To sleep but was scared that she would somehow miss her stop.
After a time, a young man squeezed in next to her.
She relaxed. Put away her book. Even smiled.
"Do you know where this bus is going?" she asked.
"Does it matter?" he replied.
And he was right. It didn't matter anymore.

Valerie

Professional comedy entertainer, genuine male 73, practising nudist, enjoys quiet times, bingo, seeks nice lady to join him for nudist clubs and good company - Personal ad in *Saga Magazine*

I am a size eight: one fat lady.
Comfortable in every square inch of my vast acreage,
I have a coastline full of coves and cliff top walks,
A rich hinterland of forests and valleys and places
Where the discerning traveller may wish to linger.
I am a lake in which you could drown yourself.

I entertain though that hardly makes me a pro.
I can raise a smile, hold a tune,
Pull a startled rabbit from a hat.

At night I skinny-dip and fatty-dip
Across the clear blue of the bedroom carpet
Or glide and swoop like an owl
With one slow slap of my bingo wings.

If you are genuine, then I too am real.
I'm not a broken puppet
Looking for discreet, no strings attached fun.
Remember indiscretion is the better part of Valerie.
So eyes down, look in
For a line, four corners or perhaps a full house.
Bingo called?

The Bibliophile Mystery

I suspect most men feel excited when they enter a brothel.
For me, an antiquarian bookshop works just as well.
Nothing can match the allure of its mustiness.
Not even the scent of a woman.

In my virgin youth, I was bewitched by surface beauty:
Moroccan-bound, hand-tooled leather, top-edge gilt
before the inevitable smutty phase kicked in.
Scouts In Bondage bought for less than the price of a second-class
stamp,
rejecting *The Day Amanda Came*, its dust-jacket being too sunned,
searching in vain for *Shag the Pony*.

Then discovering those left on the shelf:
Lawrence's *The Lost Girl*, first edition, second state, page 256 on a
cancel,
slightly foxed, like the freckles on a young lady's face.
An early Orwell, signed "Eric Blair, with thanks".
Forcing myself to rummage in the children's box, spotting
Ride A Cock Horse and other Nursery Rhymes playing hide
and seek, illustrated by Mervyn Peake, price unclipped.

Inscriptions intrigued, until I found all those scatterings
of "Merry Christmas" and "Happy Birthday", particularly involving
"My Darling Wife" as worthless as the confetti from last Saturday's
wedding.

Now I hunt for what's left tucked inside, much as a father
sneaks back to check their baby is really asleep and still breathing.
The copy of *Oscar and Lucinda* was hardly mint, barely acceptable,
despite the price, but what a pearl lay inside!

The gothic font for the restaurant's name was sufficiently
    pretentious,
the handwriting suspiciously continental, the bill for two repas proof
    positive.
Here was somebody's idea of romance. By candlelight, I fear.
Yet only a half-bottle of chablis, a clear head being called for.
All in all, this reeked of a limp attempt at seduction.

I picture the scene. The hug in the carpark held for too long.
The awkward attempt at a kiss. The slapped face.
The mumbled apology. The let's just forget it, shall we?
A flaccid failure transmuted into this expensive bookmark.

Pleased with my purchase, I nod my thanks
and, stepping outside, I smile and light a cigarette.

The Secret Life of Apples

Not enough people believe in the law of infinite possibilities.
Take Newton's apple. Or Eve's might be just as good.
Perhaps a golden apple from Hercules or even a golden delicious.
Maybe Snow White's poisoned apple would do the trick.
When the tree releases it from its spell
it tends to fall earthwards. After all
the theory of gravity is so very plausible.

Yet one day a Peasgood Nonsuch or a Tillington Court
or even a humble Granny Smith will blast off,
soar far above the treetops, blaze well beyond
where it is likely to be a danger to low-flying aircraft
before reaching the stratosphere, aflame,
and exploding into a thousand joyful pieces:
A galaxy invisible to the naked eye.

Until then I suppose we'll just have to make do with a poem.

Hutton's Unconformity

"The mind seemed to grow giddy by looking so far into the abyss of time." - John Playfair, James Hutton's companion, 1788.

It took time to find the courage to attempt the scramble
Down, the cliff path being as treacherous as a kiss.
And once down, the scramble for the words begins.
But they are as slippery as the slope. I fear the worst.
Rocks.....sharper than a serpent's tooth
Piled haphazardly like an ill-kept country churchyard,
Grey as a winter's shipping forecast, visibility poor,
Topped with pinks, like a virgin's blush.
Told you so. Words as stale as a teacher's coffee breath
Jostle for attention, just like his unmanageable class.
I pick through the jumble, knowing they are worn, second-hand,
    possibly soiled,
And yet I must make-do and mend and create
If not something beautiful, at least something I would be seen dead in.
Around the rugged rocks the ragged rascal ran.

I see and feel defeated. But, you, sir, looked
And as you looked you knew that we had been staring
Down the wrong end of the telescope all this time.
You understood what these mute blocks and slabs were trying to say:
That time itself was not a murmuring stream meandering
To nowhere in particular but an ocean.
Or rather ocean after ocean after rolling ocean stretching
Further than the mind can see. Multitudinous.
And I bet that knowledge jabbed you with all the force
Of that gannet's beak, bayoneting the waves.
High above me, swallows swoop and dive and gather
Around the ruins of the abandoned church;
Below my feet, the sea, always an attentive lover,
Relentless, timeless, licks every nook and cranny in the rocks.

I look around and see with your eyes, sir,
But I hold this pen in my own left hand and write.

Byron's Final Restless Place

I have become a patient man,
Waiting, motionless, poised,
Like the globe of ink balanced
At the end of a nib.
My fingers itch for the feel
Of a pen shaft, worn smooth by use,
Which only the scratch of words across paper can cure.
Just my mind surges like The Hellespont,
My thoughts tugged by its undertow,
Pulling me back and down.
I awoke one morning and found myself.....infamous.
Gulping and gasping, I taste again the salt water,
Sharp and tart on my tongue.
I have almost forgotten the taste of woman,
Almost.....but not quite!
My first chance took me unawares,
A bleary sentry dozing at his post.
The scraping and the chiselling,
The cracking and the stifled oaths.
And that sudden rush of clean air!
God, how good that felt!
And then the eyes pressed at the peep hole.
And their smells: sweat, stale beer and baccy,
And worst of all, the stink of reverence.
I heard their prayers
And then I heard them no more.
I did not know such things happened.
My chance, like the men, was gone.
The long, dark, grasping silence has returned.
It has taught me patience,
No easy task for a restless man.
But, like the silence, the men must come back.

My ears strain for the first hammer blow,
Imagining the echo upon echo of it.
I picture the struggle to lift the slabs.
A slice of light widening to a gap
Big enough for a man to slip through.
I can wait. I will wait. I am waiting.
And then I will be gone!

Exhibit 141: Stephens Island Wren (Extinct)

The sea and the sky were always shifting
so you ignored them. The rocks never changed,
your unknowable song becoming their soundtrack.
Passing that on had the force of instinct,
yet losing the power of flight a mere drop in a swirling ocean.
What was there to fear? Why exile yourself from Eden?

The lighthouse when it came gave the sea the finger.
Too quick for its keeper's sticks and stones,
it was his cat that did for you.
The wait. The pounce. The kill-bite.
Afterwards, a magus, he came bearing gifts as regular as the tides.

Now you preen and perch inside this shiny glass dome.
Immortality of a sort. Muted though,
your dead language blown away on the breeze.

Artist Unknown

Behind you, talking in whispers,
the curious file past
like mourners paying their respects.

You are invisible to them,
much like Banksy himself,
but not through choice.

The seawall separates you
from Banksy's stencilled satire,
sharp as any nip from a hermit crab's claws.

The queue, socially-distanced,
edges forward like an incoming tide,
few looking closely at the work itself.

Most squat, point and pose
as if finding it means
they played a part in its creation.

One woman begs her dog
to sit and stare at the camera.
It prefers to pee on the beach.

A trio of sweaty cyclists josh
about blasting it out, lugging it away,
fenced for a fortune via the dark web.

You set up your easel
then move it a few feet to the left,
like a fast bowler adjusting his field.

You always dress the same,
ignoring the weather, a refugee
or somebody in the early stages of dementia.

Stepping aside, you stand apart.
The arthritic veteran hidden on the boundary
dreading a slog dropping his way.

Getting off the mark is always the tricky bit
so no flashy strokes until you've got your eye in.
A series of dabs, a flick of the wrist.

Finally though you settle into a rhythm,
pier, prom and beach huts all emerging
as if from a lingering sea-fret.

You'll risk pricing this at three hundred.
Signed. Frame included.
All cash offers carefully considered.

Faust

Joe Faust, a pioneer of hang-gliding, came seventeenth in the high jump at the 1960 Rome Olympics.

Coming back from injury,
he tries to reconnect memory
to muscle, hoping he can trust his body.
Perhaps he can. Perhaps he can't.

He nods his head, keeping time
to a sacred song nobody else can hear,
as he visualises his approach,
each step a station of the cross.

His run-up, like life itself,
faster and faster
towards the end.

Then, take-off! Leaping, almost flying
until he straddles with supplication,
crossing the crucifix in perfect peace,
gazing down at Christ his saviour
before plunging with penitence
back into the pit, as hard as rock.

Much later he will put his trust
in a fabric wing and a prayer,
a cut-price, rip-off angel
chasing the current, climbing buzzard-like,
wondering if this is the time
his body will corkscrew back to earth,
a flailing tangle of blood and bone, wire and canvas,
freeing him to rise
into the arms of a welcoming God.

His Faustian pact honoured, fulfilled.

Down To Earth

As soon as I could walk properly
Granny taught me how to plant potatoes.
She bent to dig the hole, her back a well-oiled hinge,
then "Dip and drop, Rita, dip and drop."
I made sure the eyes were always at the top.
For weeks I was sure we were burying some poor creature alive.

"Respect the earth, Dear Rita.
She is like a mother.
All life comes from her.
We water her with our tears.
We nourish her with our blood."
At times Granny could be really frightening.

So we missed it floating down.

From nowhere, beautiful and orange,
it moved towards us, like somebody under water.
Granny grabbed my hand so tightly I almost cried.
"Run! It is The Devil. Or worse, an American spy!"

I wasn't scared though, not of such a handsome smile.
Nobody I knew smiled like that, as if he'd never stop.
And when he spoke his voice was warm
and as comforting as a bedtime story.

"I am a Soviet citizen. I need to telephone Moscow."

Granny tugged me even more but I didn't budge an inch.
I am told I was strong and stubborn for my age.
"My name is Rita," I yelled, "Where are you from?"

"My name is Yuri," he replied, "Yuri Gagarin.
And I have come from the sky."

I looked up and everything had changed.

Hanratty

It's not easy talking to a man who's going to be hanged
and he didn't make it any easier. Why should he?
No last-minute confession to settle the doubts.
Seconds later he strutted to the gallows
as if he was walking into a bar with a dubious reputation.
The signalman's lever was released, dispassionately,
freeing him to go on his short, single journey.

Now it was the domesticity that jarred,
as if he'd nipped out to place a bet
or cadge a bit of bacon from the bloke next door:
the half-finished mug of tea (strong, two sugars); his radio;
the neatly-folded pyjamas; the board set up for a game of draughts.

Afterwards, in the pit, the human pendulum slows, stops
and his last involuntary spurt seeps out,
just as a glacier melts in spring.

When we stripped his bed, the blankets were still warm,
ruffled, like a museum's model of the English Lakes.
Yet this cell was certainly no shrine
and these sheets were hardly the Turin Shroud.

Not far from here, a vital piece of evidence holds its breath.
Placed in a drawer, it plays hide and seek with the truth.
A pair of women's knickers will become a relic
or at least a fragment of the one true cross.
In time, science will prove just who had dribbled into them.
But remember, please, that science once proved that
we were orbited by the Sun, that the Earth was flat.

It will be comfort as cold as his icy-blue eyes
to know that the neck that has been snapped in all of our names
was almost without a doubt the right one.

A Cold War Incident

Tonight my American boy punched me
instead of just giving me a slap.
Tomorrow my face will be
the colour of Doctor Pepper.

I'd told him if he spent his whole life trying
he would never be as good a kisser as Anatoly
so there were grounds for what he did.

Russian boys are always angry with their women
because they are too scared to be mad at anything else
but everything makes Alka, my American boy, mad:
in Russia he had money but nothing to spend it on;
here there is lots to buy but he has no money.

Perhaps Alka would be happy living on the moon, alone.

Tonight, he called me a "blyad"- a whore,
but he would be pleased if I was just his whore.

So, I gave him sex, for free,
no charge, letting him
thrash and gasp
like some kid learning how to swim.

We fight and fight
because that's the only way
he can love
and I forgive him everything.

He says his latest two-bit job
is not worth getting dressed for.
Then, in his best Walter Cronkite voice, adds
"But one day I will be President."

I wanted to rub my cheek
but that would only set him off again.
"Yes Alka. In America everything is possible," I lie.

I am virtually asleep before he speaks again.
"I will be on the right side of history," he promised.
"I'll make you proud to be Mrs Lee Harvey Oswald."

"I'm proud now, Alka. I'm so proud now,"
and for that moment we both believed it true.

The One Everybody Will Forget

In a few short years, I will be the answer
to a quiz question only a smart-ass knows.
Or the solution to a tricky crossword clue.
Two down. One across.
Compare me to Moses seeing the Promised Land
but at least he had the bulrushes and the Tablets of Stone.
Perhaps they also serve, those who orbit and wait
and wait and wait with the meter ticking.
Guess who I had last year in the back of my capsule:
Neil and Buzz! No way. You're kidding me.
But who remembers who was driving when Kennedy got shot?

Being the loneliest man not on Earth
allows plenty of time for contemplation. No bad thing
since a spacesuit makes for challenging thumb-twiddling.
So I picture the strongest men back there
being assembled, organised into a human pyramid,
grunts and groans ever higher, calls for reinforcements,
adjusting, swaying, reaching out
towards me, flailing, before crashing
down like a felled giant redwood.

Below me, Neil and Buzz bounce around the lunar surface,
an unlikely Adam and Eve. A part of me,
(just how big a part I dare not judge) wants to tease this ship
out of its orbit and slink back home to some sort of immortality.
But like Judas who would name their boy-child Michael after that?
So I hang on, Pop waiting for his daughter to return from her first date.
For a time I will live on in the stories of colleagues, a swell guy,
and the memories of loved ones, a real family man.
For a time. But then?
Neil and Buzz have left their footprints on the Moon;
I will leave mine on air.

Still Lives

The fallen-down pigeon is as big as her doll.
The wind blows its feathers
like Mummy blows her pasta when it is too hot.
Strange how it is asleep with its eyes open wide.
Perhaps it is looking for its mummy and daddy.
She is sure they won't be long.

❁

Dad has told him all about death.
How if he was squashed by a car
he wouldn't see anybody ever again. Never.
Nothing has squashed this frog though. The opposite.
Its stomach is inflated tight, like a beach ball.
He was the first in class to shoot up his hand
when Miss had wanted a better word for blown up!
Look. Tiny flies are sliding like skaters across its eyes.
Dad had told him everything stops when you are dead,
not that he could imagine himself ever stopping.

❁

Tomorrow his surgeon with pickpocket's fingers
will deftly slice him open to have a little peek inside,
a delve around. A look-see. Nothing to get too alarmed about.
After all the stats were all in his favour. Absolutely.
So why does he lay awake, waiting to be unwrapped,
worrying what this present to himself could be?

❁

She is doing remarkably well, for her age.
Everyone tells her that: doctors, visitors, chaplains.
This is just background noise, bursts of static,
a distraction from her listening out.
Instead she stares out at a space
for beyond the ward, straining, straining
to catch the first glimpse of the gatecrasher,
that uninvited guest who spoils everyone's party.

Pushing

I don't remember the time we counted fifty four trucks
through the level crossing and I told you
it was the biggest number in the world.
Nor do I remember pushing that pram, creeping through burgled
    streets,
carrying a swag of Dad's concessionary coal
to the bloke who gave him a lift to the dogs,
pretending we were trying to lull a baby to sleep.
But you remember both. What you won't remember
is me pushing your wheelchair along the same old circuit,
even though we do this every single Sunday
As if it was some quaint religious ceremony, which perhaps it is.
It's odd what we remember. Odder still what we forget.

The Last Piece

You taught me all I know about jigsaws,
how to shepherd the straight edges
and sift through the tones of blues and greys,
turning them into clouds and cliffs and seas.
All those churches, somebody's local, a cricket pavilion.

On your tray, the thatched cottage stands unfinished,
just as it's done for the past few weeks:
the open door, roses taking shape around the eaves.
It was where you were going to live if Dad had managed
to place eight little crosses in the right eight little squares.
Not much to ask, you'd have thought,
yet every week you heard an excuse you never really understood:
how West Brom's centre forward had missed a sitter
and you knew you would have to wait another week at least.
Now you talk about heaven in much the same way.

I take your hand. Your skin feels cold and smooth
like a snake's. And like a snake you seem to be preparing
to shed something: calm, easy, natural.
You are dying like you have lived, not wanting to make a fuss.

And the jigsaw? I suppose there is always something left undone.
Someone will never find out who killed Roger Ackroyd. (It was the
    doctor.)
In sheds everywhere chisels will lose their sharpness
and brushes stiffen in pots of curdling paint.
One day I will finish it in your memory,
twirling the last piece
like the cardsharp in some black and white western saloon.

Today, though, let's just sit here holding hands,
both of us knowing that it's nearly complete.

The Ghost Of Christmas Past

All morning
he has ordered the wife to find them:
the doll for the girl, the train set for the lad.
His wife, usually a nurse, sometimes a doctor,
once the leader of a Polish fact-finding delegation,
seems powerless to help. No surprises there.
Why, she can't even find the wrapping paper.
She is ruining their Christmas. His Christmas.

At visiting time
they both arrive, as punctual as the hangman.
Despite a fresh lick of concern
newly painted on their faces,
resentment seeps through, a returning patch of damp.
They play a half-hearted game of hide and seek,
looking everywhere for a dad they know, without success.
This stranger though is playing a game of statues all by himself,
rarely blinking, barely breathing, staring into space.

3am
and it is impossible to sleep on this muggy July night,
especially with his snores ricocheting around the ward
like intermittent sniper fire.
He smiles, though, with his eyes shut tight.
Inside the rapidly-emptying auditorium of his head,
the girl gently rocks her newborn off to sleep,
the lad deals with the latest derailment.
A shocking tragedy. Few survivors.
He loves to watch the children, his children,
oblivious to the woman tidying up the wrapping paper,
folding it neatly before carefully putting it aside,
for him to start a fire with on Boxing Day morning.

Waving Goodbye

Asleep, the love bite on your neck seeps out
where the doctor's needle has French-kissed your throat.
Awake, that brain of yours is working well: a patch of paint
which has the same outline as the Isle of Wight;
making anagrams of the nurse's name-Amy Devlin.
Devil many. Manly dive. Made vinyl. Many lived.
Many lived, indeed, but will one of them be you?
At night, your body throws chiaroscuro shadows against the wall,
a femme fatale from when the world was black and white.
When we go, you grip the bed-rail like an ocean liner
and wave goodbye as dry land slips out of sight.
Back home, the grasses you gave us for the garden
will be waving, waving frantically in the wind
though nobody will be there to see them wave goodbye.

Granny Smith

Just like the apple.

A doorstop of her chocolate cake
and a glass of Tizer my reward
for enduring that glimpse of eternity
they called Sunday School.

Scheherazade of the macabre,
telling how Crippen disguised his mistress
as a boy to escape the noose
before being caught by wireless. A first.
Or George Joseph Smith (no relation)
who drowned his newly-married,
newly-insured brides in their bath.

She was no swan mating for life.
Her supervisor's job at the knitwear factory
due largely to her obliging nature. It was said.
Her wedding plans changed
after her fiancé, nipping around
with a surprise bunch of roses,
found her in bed with his brother.

Once a week she dispensed a pie,
pastry as pale as cricket whites,
meat tasting like pecked-over roadkill.
Dad said it was delicious.

To be fair, she made his life a misery
during those final bed-bound weeks.
For Dad a battle. For Mum a war.

The wicked mother-in-law, always smiling,
certainly gave the fairy tale a tweak:
forever offering a poisoned apple
to her bitterest rival,
urging her to take just one big bite.

I didn't drive home for the funeral,
Mum insisting that I needn't bother,
that I wouldn't be missing much.

Granny Smith. Just like the apple,
but apples can be such dangerous things.
Sometimes they stick in your throat.

In The End

At first a dot in my rearview mirror.
A blink later, the merest twitch of your thighs
sent you slaloming past me
before you sliced the throat of the bend.

Then forgotten as I heard about an earthquake in southern Chile
and discovered that morale amongst nurses was at an all-time low.

By the time I'd caught up with you, after a tailback of traffic,
a small crowd had already gathered, shuffling, embarrassed,
as if they were queuing outside a lap dancing club.

Once I found a blackbird that had flown into our window,
upturned on the gravel, its beak a curve of polished gold,
perfect except for the neck that flopped this way and that.
You too looked perfect, except for your neck.

Of course, the police arrived to take down statements,
"I saw it happen. He was totally buggered."
Measure the skid marks, photograph the scene.

Soon the lamppost will be camouflaged by flowers,
though it's hardly been damaged, has barely a scratch,
just in need of a quick lick of paint.

I switch off the radio as a mark of respect.
One wheel of your bike keeps on revolving
but like you, like me, it will stop in the end.

Excarnation

What had he done to merit this ceremony
at a portal between land and sea?
Was he wise or brave or both?

Splayed, he does not have long to wait.
There is always a pecking order.
First a crow, anchored to the ribcage,
tug-of-warring tubes and tendons.
Later, magpies tearing the wrapping off
to get at the main presents of heart and liver.
In darkness, owls tease out scraps,
like shrapnel from a wound.
Nothing is wasted: hair makes fine nesting material.

When I go it will be in a mid-range casket,
nothing too flash but not cheapskate either.
Pan-fried behind a slowly closing curtain,
discreet like suburban sexual infidelity
or buried deep, a forgetful pirate's treasure chest.

Afterwards, somebody will regret eating that last Scotch egg
and buy another pint, to take away the taste.

An Act of Creation

I envy the dextrous and the deft,
Those who work with the grain
In clean and confident cuts,
Each dovetail eased to perfection.

Clumsy and cack-handed
I go against the grain,
My blunt pen refusing to follow my clear instructions.
I watch as words first craze then crack,
Splintering into shards,
Embedded in the flesh, they throb
With the sharp, persistent jab of failure.
Blaming my tools, I turn away.

I envy the chisellers and chasers
Of lines, the takers of risk, the reckless
And those who refuse to tiptoe across the tightrope
But who cross with a self-assured swagger
And ignore the fact that one slip, one
Stumble, one stutter
Means the terror of a fresh start.

Chasing my lines leaves me
Breathless, hands on hips, spitting out hot phlegm,
Loitering with the limp and the lame,
Pretending like them that I've only stopped
To enjoy the view.

But, miraculously, the words do sometimes
Slide into place with a reassuring click,
Lines glide into position as if they had always been there.
This time the internal rhyme works,
And the similes fit like Cinderella's slipper.

I step back from my creation
And look down.

It is good.

Or at least not bad.

Acknowledgements

Jim Friedman

Previous publications:
- 'Togetherness' was commended in the Cannon Poets Sonnet or Not Competition (2017), judged by Liz Berry;
- 'Fayum portraits' was awarded second prize in the Poets & Players Competition (2018), judged by Pascale Petit;
- 'Rescue Greyhounds' was awarded second prize in the Lord Whisky Animal Sanctuary Competition (2018), judged by Derek Sellen;
- 'Whale' was judged Outstanding in the same competition;
- 'Escape' and 'On the canal' were selected for inclusion on the Poetry in The Waiting Room website.

Thank you to Helena Nelson at Happenstance Press for her generous input when I was writing 'Bookmark'.

I would like to thank fellow members of the Derby Stanza group for their helpful comments and encouragements and the humour and goodwill with which they are made.

Finally, a huge thank you to Ian Gouge for offering to publish this joint collection and to Dave for suggesting a joint venture.

Dave Smith

- 'Shipwrecked' chosen for Guernsey's Poems on the Move (2019), judged by Maura Dooley;
- 'Man and Boy' chosen for Guernsey's Poems on the Move (2020), judged by Simon Armitage;
- 'A Mother's Love' and 'Byron's Final Restless Place' shortlisted in the Grace Dieu Writer's Circle poetry competition (2011), judged by Joanna Bezmillian;
- 'Viking, North Utsire' and 'Still Lives' published in *New Contexts: 2*, Coverstory Books (2021);
- 'The Cup of Tea' and 'Pushing Up the Snowdrops' published in *New Contexts: 3*, Coverstory books (2022);
- 'Swiss Army Poem' chosen for Guernsey's Poems on the Move (2016), judged by Ian McMillan;
- 'Sir Had Said' and 'Inside Out' published in *New Contexts: 1*, Coverstory Books (2021);
- 'Binoculars' commended in the Torbay Open Poetry Competition (2016), judged by Sue Boyle;

- 'Little Green Apples' placed third in the Newark Poetry Society Open Competition (2012), judged by Roger Elkin;
- 'Valerie' shortlisted in the Bedford International Poetry Competition (2016), judged by Ian McEwen and published in the competition's anthology;
- 'Hutton's Unconformity' commended in the Sentinel Literary Quarterly Poetry Competition (May 2016), judged by Mandy Pannett and subsequently published in the *Sentinel Literary Quarterly* (July-September 2016);
- 'A Cold War Incident' awarded first prize in the Fosseway Writers Poetry Competition (2021), judged by Martin Grey;
- 'The One Everybody Will Forget' awarded second prize in the Fosseway Writers Poetry Competition (2020), judged by Leanne Moden;
- 'The Last Piece' published in *Acumen 94* (May 2019);
- 'Waving Goodbye' special mention in Grace Dieu Writers' Circle Poetry Competition (2012), judged by Peter Branson;
- 'An Act of Creation' shortlisted in the Grace Dieu Writers' Circle Poetry Competition (2011), judged by Joanna Bezmillian;
- 'Down To Earth' was commended in The Fosseway Writers' Poetry Competition (2022), judged by Fiona Theokritoff;
- 'The Bibliophile Mystery' was shortlisted in the Plough Prize (2022).

To Jim for accepting my modest proposal of a joint collection and for inspiring, challenging and helping me to be a better poet. Thanks Jezra.

To Ian for his perceptive and meticulous editing and for setting up Derby Stanza. Thanks Ian.

To my fellow poets in Derby Stanza for keeping me on my toes and for creating such an atmosphere of trust. Thanks everybody.

To Jane, my wife. Last but hardly least. Thanks for everything including your brilliant photograph for the cover.